LittleMissMatched's

marvelous & fabulous me
Quiz Book

50 Awesome Personality Quizzes

for Figuring Out the Who, What, and Why—of YOU!

WORKMAN PUBLISHING • NEW YORK

Library of Congress Cataloging-in-Publication Data is available.

ISBN-13: 978-0-7611-4624-7

Workman books are available at special discounts when purchased in bulk for
premiums and sales promotions as well as for fund-raising or educational use.
Special editions or book excerpts also can be created to specification.
For details, contact the Special Sales Director at the address below.

Photographs by Rafael Buchler
Illustrations by Holly Howitt

We would like to thank the following merchants
in Larchmont, NY, who kindly lent their spaces:
Beadazzled, Lorilynn's, and Nicky's Pizzeria and Restaurant

WORKMAN PUBLISHING COMPANY, INC.
225 Varick Street
New York, NY 10014-4381
www.workman.com

Printed in China

First printing June 2007

10 9 8 7 6 5 4 3 2 1

acknowledgments . . .

I wanna thank all the fabulous, marvelous, kooky, zany people who helped make *Marvelous & Fabulous Me Quiz Book* possible. They are: my bestest book doctor, nurse, and midwife David Henry Sterry; my chief of quality quiz control, Jessica Bacal; my most excellent expert on emotions, Jane Ann Staw; my illustrator extraordinaire, Holly Kowitt; my partner-in-coloration, Penelope Horcha; my sensational star specialist, Susan Wooldridge; my Titan of Tarot, Donna Sue Scissors; my maestro of all things mystical, Michael Amy Cira; my fantastic fairy godmother, Suzie Bolotin; my exceptional co-conspirator and fast friend, Raquel Jaramillo; my master marketer, Brian Belfiglio; my ATF COO, Walter Weintz; my distinguished professor of publishing, Peter Workman; my graphic design diva, Barbara Balch; my partner-in-pictures, Leora Kahn. And anyone else my brain may be forgetting but who has lent me a helpful helping hand.

contents

beginning at the beginning of you

"Know yourself." That's what ancient Greeks used to say, only they said it in Greek, of course. "To thine own self be true." That's what Shakespeare, the super-famous poet and playwright, said. But how can you be true to you if you don't even know who you are?

Hi, I'm LittleMissMatched and for as long as I can remember, I've always wanted to know who in the world I am and how who I am fits into the world. What makes me grit my teeth and roll my eyes when my sister tries to get out of doing her chores? What makes a goofy grin pop onto my face when my best friend, Jasmine, talks to me in our own secret language that nobody else can understand? Why do I get all nervous before a Spanish test, even when I know I know all the answers? Why do I like throwing pajama parties so much? Why do I love wearing mismatched socks?

Who exactly is this person called ME? And who, exactly, are YOU?

To answer these questions, I read lots and lots of books and talked to lots and lots of people. And that's how I created all these cool quizzes to help you understand the what, why, and who of you. So, if you've ever wondered "Why am I who I am?" here's your chance to find out. See what your answers say about you. Take your temper temperature. Discover what your decor is declaring. Figure out your heart's smarts. Uncover what's in your cards. And what's in your stars.

On your mark, get set, go! Find out all about marvelous, fabulous you!

the who of me

chapter one: my room

**Are you a neatnik? Or a master of messes?
See if you clean up on the cleanliness quotient.**

quiz #1

1. You clean up your room . . .

    a. On your own about once a
week.

    (b.) Only when you're forced to.

    c. There's nothing to clean
because you keep it spotless.

2. The stuff in your drawers is . . .

    (a.) Kind of folded, but not ultra-
organized.

    b. Crazy, messy, jumbly with stuff
trailing out all over.

    c. Ultra-mega-superorganized
with everything folded perfectly
and sorted into categories.

3. In your knapsack/bag . . .

    (a.) There's a lot of stuff, but you
can fish out anything—from a
paper clip to a favorite pen—
sooner or later.

    b. There's a sandwich from a
school trip you took a month
ago, that is now growing a
greenish-blue fuzz.

    c. Every pen, pencil, and note-
book is in its own separate
compartment, and not a single
scrap of paper, stick of gum, or
article of clothing is cluttering
up the inside of the bag.

4. On your desk . . .

    a. There are lots of piles of things
that might make it look a bit
cluttered, but you know where
everything is.

    (b.) What desk? There's SO much
stuff thrown all over, it has vir-
tually disappeared!

    c. There are very few items and, if
even the tiniest of those items
has been moved just a fraction
of an inch, you'll know the
moment you walk in your room.

HERE'S HOW YOU SCORED:

Mostly As: You're on top of your mess, but you're not over-the-top about it. You know how to be organized, even though it's not exactly your top priority. But, if stuff gets totally out of control, that drives you slightly loony. Since you're a bit all over the map organization-wise, you might want to think about making a cleaning schedule or spending a few minutes a day tidying up. This might help you become meltdown-free when you can't find something.

Mostly Bs: You're a master of messes (like me!). If this works for you, and you find you function best with a little bit of mess, then go crazy with the chaos! Then again, if you find yourself stressing out a lot because you can't find things when you need them, or you keep losing homework, you might want to think about making a change. Not that you're going to go crazy with the cleanup, but once a week you could make some time to sort through your mess and tidy up.

Mostly Cs: You're a bit of a neat-nik (like my sister!). Which is totally okay because you probably discovered a long time ago that having everything nice and clean makes you feel good. I know my sister says she actually LIKES making her bed because it makes her crazy to walk into her room if it's a big, nasty, unmade mess.

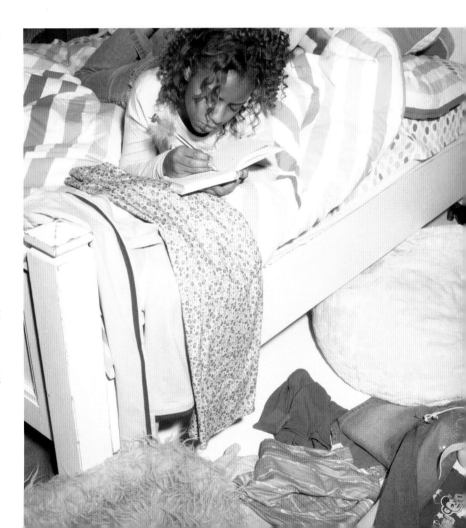

What does your room say about you?
Discover what your decor is declaring.

quiz #2

1. Your bed has . . .

    a. A blanket that belonged to your grandma, and lots of pretty, frilly pillows.

    b. Sheets and pillows that make for zany, multicolored, mismatched madness.

    c. Sheets and pillows that have calm, muted colors.

2. If you could pick any object to put in your room, you'd choose . . .

    a. An antique bureau with a fancy mirror above it.

    b. A big, fluffy, crazy-colored beanbag chair.

    c. A cute little night table that matches your walls.

3. If your room belonged to a character on a TV show, she would live . . .

    a. In the golden olden days.

    b. In a kooky cartoon.

    c. Right here, right now!

4. An interviewer, asking about your room, might say:

    a. "Do you do all your shopping in antiques stores?"

    b. "How do you combine so many different kinds of objects and colors and patterns and STILL have everything look good?"

    c. "How did you get everything in your room to match so perfectly?"

HERE'S HOW YOU SCORED:

Mostly As: You definitely like the pretty, old-fashioned look of antiques and lace. Maybe you like old movies, too. And you might find yourself drawn to flea markets and garage sales because they're full of stuff no one makes anymore but you think is so cool, like typewriters and record players.

Mostly Bs: You're eclectic and proud! You march to your own drummer and you're not afraid to mix and match colors and style, and you pull it off with panache. You're probably drawn to all different kinds of stuff. You see possibilities where others dare not dream. Even if you're not an artist, you're definitely into making a statement—and you don't let the trendazoids cramp your singular style!

Mostly Cs: You favor the contemporary look you see in magazines and on TV shows. When you look at catalogs with room decor, you wouldn't mind having everything on that page because you like how it goes together so perfectly. Just watch your pocketbook, cuz your allowance probably isn't gonna cover the stuff you covet.

Are you an early bird or a night owl?
Find out what time zone your clock is set to.

quiz #3

1. When your alarm clock goes off in the morning . . .

    a. What alarm? I'm up with the sun.

    b. I hit snooze once, and then I'm up and at it.

    c. I hit snooze. I hit it again. And again. And again. And again. Then my family has to literally drag me out of bed.

2. The morning sun shining through my window . . .

    a. Blankets me in a warm and happy glow.

    b. Is a little too bright, but reminds me it's time to get up.

    c. Is my dreaded enemy. I bury my head under the covers to hide from it.

3. It's time to go to bed when . . .

    a. It's my bedtime. That's at the same time every night—never too late. I don't like feeling tired the next day.

    b. I get sleepy, whether it's early or late.

    c. When everyone else in my house—in fact, my entire part of the world—is asleep.

4. My favorite time of day is . . .

    a. The top of the morning.

    b. When I'm having fun.

    c. Right at night.

HERE'S HOW YOU SCORED:

Mostly As: You are the definition of a morning person. You like getting up early. You like feeling ahead of the game. You probably get a lot done in the first half of the day, but start to conk out by the end. And if you're like most early birds, you find yourself rising and shining early—even on weekends!

Mostly Bs: Okay, you're not exactly an early bird, but you've made peace with your A.M. alarm. On weekdays, you're okay about being woken up for school, but on weekends you like to sleep in. Mornings make your brain feel a little like thick, mushy oatmeal. Fortunately, it doesn't take too much time after you wake up to get your engine up and running.

Mostly Cs: You're a night owl. You don't give a hoot for mornings: In fact, you wish there was no such thing! You don't start feeling really awake until the sun's gone down, but then, once your juices are revved—you're ready to rock all night long. You are a creature of the night. That's when you're most creative, most inspired, and wackiest!

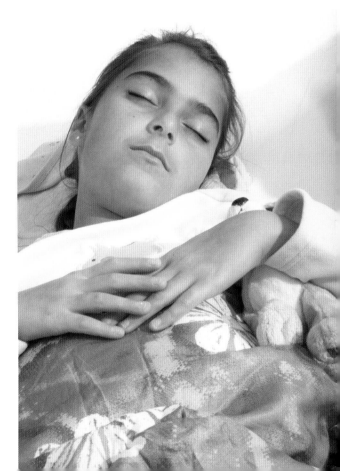

Are your walls a blank slate or a clutter of collages?
Your walls talk—figure out what they're saying!

quiz #4

1. Your walls are . . .

a. Covered with photographs of everyone you love, as well as pictures and/or posters of your favorite actors, actresses, bands, etc.

b. Covered with your own drawings, paintings, and stuff you made in school.

c. Pretty bare.

2. If a friend walks into your room and starts a sentence with "Wow," the rest of the sentence might be . . .

a. "I can't believe you still have this wacky picture of me on your bulletin board."

b. "Did you paint that picture yourself?"

c. "I need to buy you a poster!"

3. If you could do your walls over again, you would . . .

a. Why do them all over? Just add MORE photos and posters!

b. Paint a mural on the biggest one.

c. Spackle the nail holes and paint all the walls white.

4. If you could have just one thing hanging on your wall, it would be . . .

a. A precious photo of someone you love.

b. A mirror.

c. One thing? That's too much!

Mostly As: Your walls are there to give a shout-out to family, friends, and people you admire. You love to be reminded of the people close to you. They inspire you! They make a smile break out all over your face. And when you feel a little blue, you can stare at the pics of your peeps and perk right up.

Mostly Bs: You're so creative, you inspire yourself! That's right: You enjoy seeing the fruits of your labor all around you. You like keeping your creative juices flowing at all times, even when you're about to fall asleep. I bet that sometimes your mind is racing so fast with so many projects, you have a hard time falling asleep!

Mostly Cs: You have a minimalist approach to room decor that probably reflects your inner calm. You don't feel the need to have your whole life displayed because, for you, it's all about what's inside. You're just as creative as As and Bs, but you don't wear it on your sleeve—or on your walls!

What would your perfect room look like?

quiz #5

What colors would you paint your ideal room?

_____

_____

What would be hanging on your walls?

_____

_____

How would you decorate it? Would it be sleek and modern or like an old-fashioned country inn? Tell me!

_____

_____

_____

_____

Can you decorate your perfect room? Color this in, adding as many mismatched patterns as you'd like! Clutter up the walls or leave them blank: It's up to you!

chapter two: my clothes

Are you a true blue or do you swoon for maroon?
Find out your spot on the color wheel.

quiz #6

1. Your favorite gemstone of the three below is:
- a. Turquoise.
- b. Ruby.
- c. Emerald.

2. A dress in your favorite color makes you feel:
- a. Calm, cool, and collected.
- b. Wild, crazy, and passionate.
- c. Down-to-earth, easygoing, and natural.

3. A room in your favorite color makes you feel like:
- a. Chilling out.
- b. Getting cozy or having a party.
- c. Going outside.

4. Your favorite colors make you think about:
- a. Water, the sky.
- b. Roses, tomatoes.
- c. Forests, a pebbled brook.

HERE'S HOW YOU SCORED:

Mostly As: You love cool colors like blues and purples. These colors make you feel serene. Mellow blues and calm moods suit you just fine.

Mostly Bs: You love warm colors like reds and oranges. You're a bit of a drama queen. But that's okay, you're also a very warm person. You like to hug and be hugged.

Mostly Cs: You love the outdoors. You love neutral, earthy colors like greens, beiges, and browns. Being in the woods, walking through a field, or swimming in a pond are your idea of FUNFUNFUN.

**Are you a fashionista or a fashion-not-a?
Rate where you sit on the best-dressed list.**

quiz #7

1. When you see a fashion magazine, you . . .

   a. Grab it and settle down for a fashion feast, poring over every detail of every dress and accessory as if your life depends on it.

   b. Roll your eyes and shake your head because you honestly couldn't care less.

   c. Think, "Maybe I'll read it for the articles."

2. Going shopping for clothes is . . .

   a. Your idea of heavenly bliss.

   b. About as much fun as going to a dentist with a mean streak.

   c. Fun if you go directly to the kind of clothing store you like and shop for something specific.

3. To play YOU in a movie, a character would have to wear clothes that were . . .

   a. Straight off the runway: fancy and trendy.

   b. Straight off the back of a truck: comfortable and loose.

   c. Straight out of a catalog: Stylish and right down the middle.

4. Among your friends, you're the one who . . .

   a. Always has—or wants—the latest and greatest clothes.

   b. Has zero interest in what you—or anyone else—is wearing.

   c. Wears clothes that just kind of fit, and fit in.

HERE'S HOW YOU SCORED:

Mostly As: All hail the fashionista supreme! Let's face it: You LOVE your clothes, you like looking good, and you pay a lot of attention to details. You're a trailblazer when it comes to fashion. But beware: Don't get caught in the trap of thinking you are what you wear! A REAL fashionista can wear yesterday's jeans with last season's sweater—and still make it look right off the runway!

Mostly Bs: Clothes are NOT where it's at for you. If you could, you'd wear your favorite outfit over and over again till the cows came home. Yours is the straightforward approach. You want clothes that are no fuss and no nonsense and don't get in the way. You don't run with the pack and this takes self-confidence because it's tough bucking trends!

Mostly Cs: You do care about how you look but you're not interested in attracting a lot of attention, either. In fact, what's most important to you is that you fit in. You don't judge other people by what they wear, though. As far as clothes go, you totally believe in "live and let live."

**Are you a tomboy or a girly girl?
Understand who inspires your style.**

quiz #8

1. You love getting dressed for . . .

   a. A sporting event.

   b. A dress-up party.

   c. A day with your friends just hanging out.

2. Your dream outfit would include . . .

   a. The newest, coolest sneakers.

   b. A flowing ballgown.

   c. Your best friend's jeans.

3. Your style icon is . . .

   a. A famous athlete.

   b. A glamorous actress.

   c. The girl at school who is known for having all the latest fashions.

4. You hate . . .

   a. Dressing up.

   b. Dressing down.

   c. Dressing for something when you don't know what other people will be wearing.

HERE'S HOW YOU SCORED:

Mostly As: You like your sports, girl! You want to be comfortable and ready to jump into a game any time of the day. You're not out to impress other people with your style, but you have the latest and greatest sportswear out there.

Mostly Bs: Ballerinas, princesses, and the glitterati are your fashion icons. You like things pretty, frilly, and super-girly. Satins, silks, and petticoats are your style. And there's nothing you like more than dressing up for a party. If you could, you'd have a different gown for every day of the year.

Mostly Cs: You are a bit of a fashion chameleon. Your fashion sense is still evolving as you experiment with different looks. One week you're into skirts with stylish boots, the next you're all about torn jeans and unlaced sneakers. It's not that you're not into clothes, because you are, but you may not have found your own distinct fashion muse—yet. And you can't be put in a style box.

**What do your clothes reveal about you?
Find out if you take the disguise prize!**

quiz #9

1. Your favorite outfit . . .

   a. Reflects the true you, whatever that may be.

   b. Is totally hip: All the stars are wearing it.

   c. Is completely unique and makes its own fashion statement.

2. Wearing a school uniform would be . . .

   a. Fine because you'll figure out a way to make it work for you.

   b. Hard because school uniforms aren't exactly known for being runway material.

   c. Awful because you couldn't express your personal fashion sense, and it wouldn't let you stand out from the crowd.

3. Your favorite stores are . . .

   a. Boutiques with interesting, well-made items.

   b. Department stores stocked full of the latest fashions and designer labels.

   c. Thrift stores, secondhand boutiques, vintage-clothing stores.

4. When you get dressed in the morning you look for an outfit . . .

   a. That matches your mood that day.

   b. Most like the one you saw your favorite actress wearing on TV the other day.

   c. That will be even more outrageous than the one you wore the day before.

Mostly As: Your clothes reflect who you really are. In fact, people would use the same words to describe your wardrobe as your personality. That's why your clothes add to your confidence and make you feel special.

Mostly Bs: Your clothes are more about what's going on around you than in you. So the first impression you make may not reveal the real you. What you wear may even make people think you're someone very different from who you are. That can be nice because you're always surprising people, but it can also be hard because first impressions are tough to erase.

Mostly Cs: You consider your clothes your costume. They make a statement about what part you play on the stage of your world. You're decidedly antifashion. That's not to say you don't have your own unique style. But you want to stand out from the crowd. The question is, does your costume hide the true you? Or does it say to the world "Here I am, deal with it!"

What's your fashion favorite?

quiz #10

Describe your favorite outfit.

_____

_____

_____

What kind of clothes do you look best in?

_____

_____

_____

Do you have a favorite accessory you just can't do without,
like a hat or scarf? Do you have a favorite pair of shoes?

_____

_____

Can you draw the perfect outfit—on me?

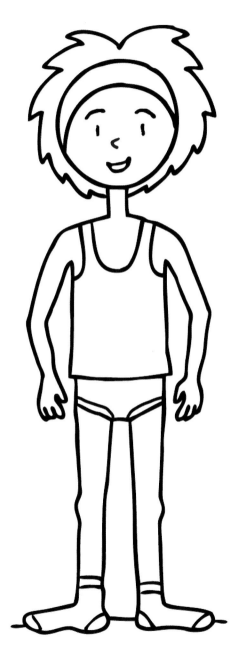

chapter three: **my friends**

Do you play follow-the-leader?
Unveil your group dynamic.

quiz #11

1. The last time you were asked to be the leader of a group, you . . .
    a. Loved it.
    b. Hated it but did okay.
    c. Hated it and stunk at it.

2. You're happiest when you're . . .
    a. Part of a big team.
    b. Part of a little committee.
    c. Doing things on your own.

3. Friends think of you as . . .
    a. The one person who can get them to do anything.
    b. Someone who's up for everything.
    c. Someone who has fun doing your own thing.

4. When faced with a problem, you . . .
    a. Go into action mode.
    b. Go to your teacher, parents, or friends for advice.
    c. Work it out in your mind before you do anything.

HERE'S HOW YOU SCORED:

Mostly As: You're a natural-born leader. You can get groups of people excited about things, and in a pinch everyone looks to you for what to do. You may be a bit impulsive at times, following your guts over your head. Guts are great, but be careful to look before you leap, especially if you're standing on the edge of something.

Mostly Bs: Being the boss and telling people what to do isn't for you. What you are is a great collaborator. You like working on a team and don't mind having someone else in charge. When someone gives you something to do, you like that everyone can completely count on you to do it.

Mostly Cs: You're way independent. Being part of a group isn't always your thing. You like to be able to solve stuff on your own, and don't like having to depend on other people. You like to think things out before you do them.

Are you a lone wolf or a pack animal? Calculate your friends factor.

quiz # 12

1. At school, there's a good chance you can be found . . .

    a. Flying solo or with your BFF.

    b. With a couple of your tried-and-true friends.

    c. Hanging with a huge group.

2. At a big party, you would most likely . . .

    a. Get a little frustrated because it's hard to have a *real* conversation with anyone.

    b. Stake out a quiet place to sit and chill with a few fun pals.

    c. Be happy as a fish in water, talking with anyone and everyone.

3. Spending time by yourself . . .

    a. Is mad fun.

    b. Is okay if it's not too much time.

    c. Makes you a bit blue.

4. How many really, really close friends do you have?

    a. Just one BFF.

    b. Two to four.

    c. Five or more.

why not try to widen that inner circle a bit and make a few new friends this year? I dare you!

Mostly Bs: You like running in a small pack with some nice pals. Sometimes group dynamics make you a little crazy, though, like when you have to keep track of who's mad at who, and stuff like that. That's why WHO is in your small circle of friends is really important to you, because if someone's not nice it can throw everything way off. And besides, who has time for NOT nice? Not ME!

Mostly Cs: You like the excitement and energy that comes with being a part of a big buzzing group. You're adventurous by nature, and don't mind exploring new friendships that might make other people look and go, "Huh?!" This, of course, can be good or bad (depending on the friends you choose), but meeting new people keeps you feeling energized.

HERE'S HOW YOU SCORED:

Mostly As: You enjoy quality alone-time as well as one or two close friendships. You've probably had the same BFF since you were little. Because you like being in the comfort zone of your best buds, you may be missing opportunities to meet new people and let new friends into your inner circle. So

Are you the class clown or the teacher's pet?
Discover what the part you play says about your need to succeed.

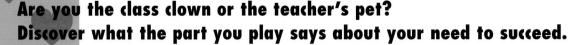

1. When you hear "substitute teacher," you think:

    a. Time to be extra helpful.

    b. Time to have fun.

    c. Time to cut class (the teacher won't notice anyway!).

2. Your best friend would describe you as . . .

    a. A serious student who'll do whatever it takes to get good grades.

    b. A bit of a class clown who'll do whatever it takes to get a laugh.

    c. Not really into school that much.

3. The last time you got in trouble at school . . .

    a. Was never.

    b. Your principal said, "You again?"

    c. Your principal said, "Are you new here?"

4. If you score an 85 on a test, you . . .

    a. Get really, really bummed because it's not 100!

    b. Get happy because that's pretty good for you.

    c. Think, "whatever," because you hadn't studied anyway.

HERE'S HOW YOU SCORED:

Mostly As: You take school mega-seriously and you're proud of it. You have a need to succeed that probably goes beyond getting good grades. You have a quest to be the best, a drive to thrive. But watch out: Sometimes your desire to be at the top can make it hard to appreciate what you've actually accomplished.

Mostly Bs: Okay, party girl: I know who you are! You're the class cutup, the girl that makes everyone go giggly. You've gotten in trouble so much it hardly even matters to you, because in your mind, school's all about having fun. But beware, all that goofing off can catch up with you. It's good you're having fun, but keep it under control. You gotta know where the line is because you don't want to go so far that you can't get back.

Mostly Cs: You're a bit of a puzzle. You could probably be the best student around, but you just don't apply yourself. You're fine with doing "fine" but don't ever push yourself to be more. It might be good to look for something you really love to do, instead of cruising along not doing everything every-one expects you to do.

Who makes your eyes light up and who makes you wanna pull your hair out? Find out what your friends and enemies reveal about you.

quiz #14

1. You and your best friend . . .

    a. Come from pretty similar backgrounds.

    b. Couldn't have more different backgrounds.

    c. Are in the very same family.

2. It really bothers you when . . .

    a. People disagree with you.

    b. Everyone thinks and acts the same way.

    c. Someone teases a member of your family.

3. When you have a delicious secret, you're tempted to . . .

    a. Spill it to your best friend.

    b. Whisper it to someone you hardly know.

    c. Confide in your mom.

4. Try to imagine fifteen years from now. You and your best friend will be . . .

    a. Living in the same neighborhood.

    b. Who knows? I'll have another best friend by then.

    c. Spending holidays together.

HERE'S HOW YOU SCORED:

Mostly As: You're drawn to people who think like you, talk like you, dress like you, eat like you. You know where you stand with your friends and you don't like to be surprised by the unexpected. Problem is, you can be a tad too wary of someone just because they're a bit different from you, so you might want to try to open your heart to other kinds of people—you may be in for a nice surprise!

Mostly Bs: You know how they say opposites attract? Well, that's you in a nutshell. You love to meet different kinds of people who have totally different takes on the world. You're comfortable with the unfamiliar, and you crave new ideas, new places, new routines. In fact, you're so into what's different that you tend to turn up your nose at anyone who reminds you of you!

Mostly Cs: You're lucky because when you're looking for a friend, all you've gotta do is walk into the living room. Your friends are right in your very own family. Just remember, it can be fun to have friends outside your clan, too. Try not to cut yourself off from meeting new people. There's a whole fabulous, marvelous, kooky, zany world out there!

What's the greatest thing about having great friends?

quiz # 15

What is the name of your very best friend?
If you have more than one, list them all:

_____

_____

_____

_____

What's the best thing your best friend has ever
done for you?

_____

_____

_____

_____

What's the best thing you've ever done for her?

_____

_____

_____

What are your favorite things to do with your friends?

_____

_____

_____

Who would you like to be friends with who you only kinda know now?

_____

_____

_____

chapter four: my moods

**Are you a roller coaster or an easy glider?
Take your temper temperature.**

quiz #16

1. After a bad day at school, you . . .
   a. Totally avoid your friends and family.
   b. Chill out after yakking to your friends about it.
   c. Shrug a "whatever" and enjoy the rest of your day.

2. A weather report about you would say . . .
   a. Chance of thunderstorms and lightning.
   b. Blue skies, then partly cloudy.
   c. Sunny, sunny, sunny.

3. Your big weekend movie plan with friends gets canceled, and you're disappointed. You are most likely to . . .
   a. Have a miserable weekend because you just won't let it go.
   b. Sulk around for a little while, but then get over it.
   c. Bounce back quickly and make another plan.

4. When you compare yourself to friends, you think . . .
   a. I'm the moodiest human being I know.
   b. I'm just about as moody as everyone else.
   c. Everybody's moodier than me.

Mostly As: If you were a carnival ride, you'd be the roller coaster. Up, down, inside, and out, your moods can exhaust you! That's why it'd be a good idea to have some kind of escape for yourself. I have a journal where I like to blow off steam. And my best friend, Jasmine, has me!

Mostly Bs: There are days where you can go from happy to grumpy pretty easily, but you also know how to snap yourself out of a bad mood. When you're down, it helps

What splits your sides and tickles your fancy?
Find out what kind of funny your funny bone is.

quiz # 17

1. You're sure to exercise your funny bone when . . .

    a. Your frenemy slips on some Jell-O and falls flat on her butt.

    b. Someone tells you a really cool riddle or joke.

    c. You thumb through your favorite comic books.

2. You can't keep yourself from laughing when . . .

    a. Someone farts.

    b. Someone does a clever impersonation of one of your teachers.

    c. You watch an episode of SpongeBob—even if you've seen it a million times.

3. Your best friend would say you're . . .

    a. A bit of a belly laugher.

    b. More of a titterer, though you actually don't laugh a lot.

    c. A total giggler because you laugh at just about anything.

4. The following would be funny ONLY if it happened to someone else:

    a. Accidentally knocking the top of an ice-cream cone off and having it plop onto the sidewalk.

    b. Mispronouncing a word.

    c. Drawing a dog that everyone thinks is a horse.

HERE'S HOW YOU SCORED:

Mostly As: You love to laugh—loud! And nothing makes you laugh harder and louder than clowns falling down, getting smacked around, or taking a pie in the face. It's not what they *say* that hits your funny bone so hard, but what they *do*. Physical comedy is your thing and you love to watch it and make it.

Mostly Bs: No one's going to hear you laughing from across a room, but that doesn't mean you don't love a great joke. It's just that you're more an appreciator of good humor than a laugh-out-loud sort of girl. You've got a big brain that loves puns and complicated, wordy jokes. And your sense of humor is very grown-up.

Mostly Cs: You're a grandmaster giggler. And it's your eyes that tell you what's funny. You get all goofy when you look at stuff that's silly, nutty, or off-kilter. The funny papers and toonz are your comedy cup of tea. But you'll also bust a gut when you see things that look interestingly weird or strangely silly.

Are you an Eeyore or a Little Mary Sunshine?
Find out if you see the world as half-full or half-empty.

quiz #18

1. When you find the prize inside a cereal box, you . . .

   a. Dig it out and say, "What a dinky rip-off!"

   b. Leave it unopened so that someone else in your family can find it.

   c. Open it when you finally get to that part of the cereal box, and keep it even though it's only a plastic toy because "Hey, a prize is a prize."

2. You wake up most days . . .

   a. On the wrong side of the bed, a grumbly grumpus.

   b. Smack dab in the middle of the bed—in a decently decent mood.

   c. On the right side of the bed— in a mucho good mood.

3. When a friend disappoints you, you think:

   a. I KNEW this was gonna happen.

   b. I didn't think this would EVER happen.

   c. It'll be fine: She'll apologize later.

4. When everything is going your way . . .

   a. You look out for what's about to go wrong.

   b. You're kinda surprised.

   c. You're psyched because, hey, that's how it should be.

HERE'S HOW YOU SCORED:

Mostly As: You always have the feeling that something's about to go wrong. Even when you try, you can't help but dwell on the bad stuff that could happen—ANY SECOND! This keeps you from ever REALLY enjoying stuff AS it happens. It might be good for you to have a glass-half-full pal, someone who sees how positively great the world is. And maybe experiment with making a list of things to be happy about in your life.

Mostly Bs: You don't go around with a lot of expectations one way or the other. You're a realist. You hope for the best but you're ready for the worst. You're not too up, not too down. You're right in the middle!

Mostly Cs: You're a true optimist. You expect all will go swimmingly! And even when it doesn't, you expect things will get better soon enough. It's great to believe that it's all gonna be good, but make sure you try to see yourself and the world as they *really* are instead of what you want them to be—at least every once in a while.

Are you juice or soda?
Uncap your bubblocity.

quiz #19

1. When you're totally stoked to see a friend, you . . .

  a. Give her a big wraparound hug.

  b. Give her a little kiss on the cheek.

  c. Smile and say, "Hey."

2. When you're stuck inside on a rainy day . . .

  a. You go totally crazy climbing the walls.

  b. You're tickled because there's tons of fun stuff to do in the house.

  c. You'll probably lie on your bed for a few hours, staring at your ceiling—daydreaming your afternoon away.

3. Friends think you're . . .

  a. A little hyper.

  b. Sweet and easygoing.

  c. Almost too mellow.

4. If you were a kind of music, you'd be . . .

  a. Hip-hop.

  b. Rock.

  c. Easy listening.

Mostly As: You are a high-caffeine drink. You're ON—almost all of the time. You like to do stuff in a BIG way. And while you're super-fun to be with, you can also be a little overwhelming at times. So make sure you're not bubbling over onto those less sparkly than you.

Mostly Bs: You're a fruit seltzer: fizzy and fun. You're game for most things, and you're up for new challenges. But you also know how to lay low. That's why people love being around you—because you know how to fit right in and you've got amazing blendability.

Mostly Cs: You're a mellow cup o' tea. You don't mind taking it nice and easy, steady as she goes. The only trouble is, sometimes it's hard to get you to get up and go! But with a little juice from others, you're a grand pal who lets everyone be who they want to be.

What's your notion of emotion?

quiz #20

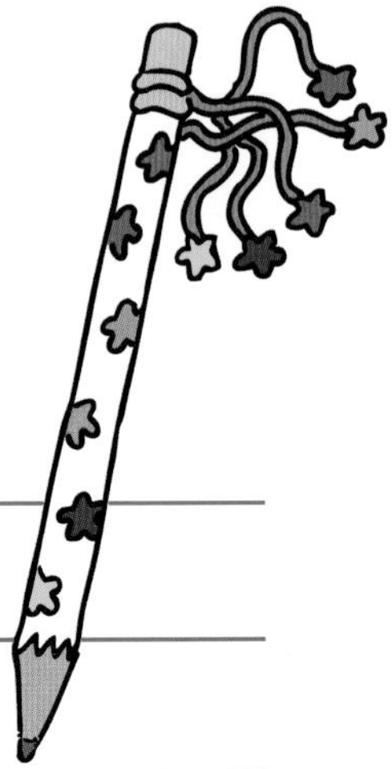

What makes you laugh so hard you nearly pee?

_____

_____

_____

What makes you cry until you're all cried out?

_____

_____

_____

What kind of stuff makes you grin from ear to ear?

_____

_____

_____

What makes you mad as a sack of cats?

_____

_____

_____

What makes you bluer than the sky?

_____

_____

_____

If you had to choose the happiest moment in your life, what would it be?

_____

_____

_____

_____

_____

chapter five: my adventures in eating

Are you a comfort-food fanatic or a try-anything explorer? Understand how safe your taste buds play it.

quiz #21

1. A great new ethnic restaurant just opened with all kinds of foods you never tried before. You . . .

    a. Can hardly wait to go and try everything on the menu!

    b. Avoid it like the plague.

2. Becoming a really great cook is . . .

    a. Super-important to you.

    b. At the bottom of your life's To-Do list. Fast food is fine with you.

3. If you could, you'd . . .

    a. Go to the fanciest five-star restaurant in the world for dinner every night.

    b. Eat pizza or burgers seven nights, seven days a week.

4. Food is something you . . .

    a. Love and think about even when it's not time for a meal.

    b. Eat when you're hungry.

HERE'S HOW YOU SCORED:

Mostly As: You're an adventurous gourmand, a foodie, a lover of the whole world's table. You know that good food isn't just about putting stuff in your mouth and swallowing. It's about giving your taste buds an adventure and letting your senses go wild. Maybe you should start thinking about becoming a chef, food critic, or cookbook editor!

Mostly Bs: When it comes to food, you like what you like, and you don't see the point of trying new stuff. You're a bit picky about food, too. That's okay, but you might be pleasantly surprised by how many things you've never tasted that you actually might like. So try something new every now and again, okay?

What do you crave at snack time?
Open up your cupboard for this taste test.

quiz #22

1. If you could bring just one food with you to a deserted island, it would be . . .

    a. Potato chips.

    b. Candy.

    c. Spicy beef jerky.

    d. Bread.

2. Your mouth waters just thinking about . . .

    a. French fries.

    b. Chocolate cake with ice cream.

    c. Tacos with the works.

    d. Buttered noodles.

3. You're at the movies and have only enough money to buy one thing. You choose . . .

    a. A bag of popcorn.

    b. Twizzlers.

    c. Nachos with the spicy cheese sauce.

    d. A soft pretzel (preferably unsalted).

4. The condiment you crave is . . .

    a. Salt.

    b. Sugar.

    c. Salsa.

    d. You hate condiments.

Mostly As: You're silly for salt! And you'd take salty over sweet any day of the week. Did you know that salt was once so treasured, it was actually used as money back in ancient times? That's right—people were paid for a hard day's work in salt! That's where the word "salary" comes from. As yummy (and valuable!) as salt is, you shouldn't overdo it. Too much salt will make your body unhappy.

Mostly Bs: Hello, Miss Sweet Tooth! Sweet things make your heart sing. Did you know that in ancient Persia, how to make sugar was a closely guarded state secret? Crazy huh?! I'm sure you already know sugar isn't good for you. Just remember your last trip to the dentist? Ouch!

Mostly Cs: Spice is twice as nice with you! You like putting your taste buds into overdrive! I'll bet you crave Indian, Thai, and Mexican food. It's a good thing you didn't live a long time ago because spices, like salt, were once so precious that people risked their lives to buy and sell them. Now all you gotta do is go to the supermarket. Lucky you!

Mostly Ds: You like your food on the bland side. Hey, it's not that you don't have an adventurous part of you, it's just not located in your mouth. If you could choose, you'd eat things that are just white or beige. Greens, red, purples, and oranges tend to turn your stomach. Here's the thing: Every color food has different nutrients. So the more colors you eat (and I'm not talking artificially colored, here), the healthier you'll be!

Do you chew with your mouth open or do you always reach for your napkin first? Gauge your manners meter.

quiz #23

1. Here is how you set the table:

    a. Fork on left on top of napkin, spoon and knife on the right.

    b. Forks. Plates. Napkins. Good to go.

    c. You wish you knew . . .

2. When you want salt and it's across the table, you say:

    a. "Excuse me, would you please pass the salt?"

    b. You point and say, "Hand me that, will ya?"

    c. You just reach for it.

3. Licking your fingers . . .

    a. Should never be done at a table.

    b. Can be done discreetly at a table.

    c. Should be done whenever you like: If the food was good, why not show it?

4. When your host at a dinner party offers you a food that you don't like you . . .

    a. Accept a portion and eat it because you don't want to insult your host.

    b. Accept a portion and at least *try* to eat it, but leave most of it.

    c. Say, "That stuff? You must be joking."

HERE'S HOW YOU SCORED:

Mostly As: Your manners are A-plus! Are you, like, royalty or something? And the nice thing about having good manners is that people will always invite you back. Like, I know my best friend Jasmine's mom loves it when I tell her how awesome her cooking is. And that's why I always get asked over for dinner again and again!

Mostly Bs: You have perfectly decent manners. Sometimes you can be a little clueless, but there are certainly worse things to be. And hey, you're trying to learn. As long as you say your pleases and thank-yous, you'll do just fine.

Most Cs: Wow—you better sign up right now for Miss Manners! Here's the thing: Good manners aren't just about where to put the knife and fork or how to fold a napkin. It's about letting the people around you know you appreciate them. After all, it doesn't take a lot to say "please" and "thank you," does it?!

Are you a kitchen magician or a culinary catastrophe?
Find out if you're really cooking.

quiz #24

1. Cookbooks are . . .

    a. Unnecessary, since you can cook anything without one.

    b. Essential because you can't cook without one.

    c. Not nearly as good as a phone book (because you can use a phone book to order takeout).

2. The kind of food you cook is . . .

    a. Whatever you're inspired to invent.

    b. The kind of food someone can give you a good recipe for.

    c. Invisible.

3. Cumin . . .

    a. Is great in curries.

    b. That's a spice, right?

    c. Rhymes with human. That's all you know about it.

4. A broiler is great for . . .

    a. Toasting nuts, melting goat cheese on slices of baguette, grilling asparagus.

    b. Making an awesome grilled cheese or making toast when the toaster's broken.

    c. Something other people use.

HERE'S HOW YOU SCORED:

Mostly As: Everyone's coming to your house for dinner tonight, because you're an awesome cook! You naturally know what ingredients will taste deeelish together. You may be destined to become a famous chef!!!

Mostly Bs: You are totally competent in the kitchen. It's not that you have a flair for cooking, but you can do it well when you have to, and things taste good enough when you cook.

Mostly Cs: Cooking is just not your thing, but you might wanna learn how to make at least a few things before you grow up and leave home, because having only toast and butter will get kind of boring after a while, don't ya think?!

What's your ideal meal?

quiz #25

What are your top five favorite foods?

1. _____

2. _____

3. _____

4. _____

5. _____

What are your five least favorite foods?

1. _____

2. _____

3. _____

4. _____

5. _____

What is your favorite dessert?

_____

_____

What is your favorite drink?

_____

_____

What is your favorite snack?

_____

_____

The worst meal you've ever had was:

_____

_____

The best meal you've ever had was:

_____

_____

chapter six: my favorite things to do

Are you a rock climber or a web surfer? See what the stuff you do says about you.

quiz #26

1. When you're in front of your computer, you like to . . .
- a. Research cool places for off-road biking.
- b. Play a challenging game.
- c. Chat with friends.
- d. Play around with photographs you've taken.

2. Your ideal day would have to include . . .
- a. A lot of physical activity.
- b. Reading a book.
- c. At least a few of your friends.
- d. Painting or drawing.

3. Friends think of you as a person who uses your free time to do things that are . . .
- a. Athletic.
- b. Brainy.
- c. Social.
- d. Artistic.

4. Rocks are for . . .
- a. Climbing.
- b. Earth science research.
- c. Sitting on with friends.
- d. Drawing.

HERE'S HOW YOU SCORED:

Mostly As: You use free time to get out and get active. Even if you're not into competitive sports, you're still athletic. You probably like to hike and hang out in nature, too.

Mostly Bs: In your free time, you like to think long and hard about things. You enjoy being alone with your thoughts. You can always be found with a book, a puzzle, or a pen and notebook, jotting stuff down.

Mostly Cs: Your free time allows you to unleash the social butterfly in you. Hanging out with friends and family is what makes you happiest. You're drawn to parties, gatherings, the telephone, and you're probably a major IMer. R U? How gr8!

Mostly Ds: You live for arts-and-crafts projects. You love to draw, paint, photograph, sew, glue, create. You've got a mega-imagination and you're always thinking up new, cool things you can make.

Are you mad for math or haywire for history?
School yourself on school.

quiz #27

1. Zero is a cool number because . . .

    a. It's an ancient invention.

    b. It lets us write big numbers.

    c. Zero change in a lab experiment means you get to start a new one.

    d. A character with zero friends is going to be fun to read about.

2. Your favorite type of books have . . .

    a. Stories about the past.

    b. Numbers and equations.

    c. Cool experiments and inventions.

    d. An engrossing story.

3. When you think of numbers, you automatically think of . . .

    a. The dates of historical events.

    b. Adding, subtracting, etc.

    c. Laboratory notations.

    d. Knowing what page you're on.

4. If you could have dinner with one famous person in history, it would be . . .

    a. Marco Polo, so he could regale you with stories of his trips around the world in olden times.

    b. Erno Rubik, the inventor of the Rubik's Cube, so he could show you how to use numerical sequences to solve the puzzle!

    c. Albert Einstein, so you could hear the Theory of Relativity from the horse's mouth.

    d. William Shakespeare, so he could recite his sonnets for you, and wax on about his plays.

HERE'S HOW YOU SCORED:

Mostly As: History makes you happy. You like reading about far away and long ago. And you like to think about how those places made your life the way it is now. You also probably enjoy traveling because you dig seeing all the different ways other people live.

Mostly Bs: You're mad for math. Numbers are your thing, and you have a real feel for the way mathematical principles work. You're probably pretty analytical in general, and are good at figuring things out in your head. You especially like the logic and order of math. The fact that 2 x 2 is always 4 comforts you.

Mostly Cs: You're psyched about science. You love conducting experiments and observing things. You're curious about the natural world, and how things interact with one another. You like to think about how the universe was created, and sometimes your questions have no answers. And that's good, because for scientists, questions are as important as answers.

Mostly Ds: You're a reader and writer all the way. You love English and poetry. And you know how to make up a great yarn. You've got a vivid imagination and you think creatively: In fact, it's the only way you know how to think.

**Do you crave comedy or care to be scared?
See what tricks your flicks can show you.**

quiz #28

1. You like it best when movies give you . . .

    a. An adrenaline rush.

    b. A good laugh.

    c. A good scare.

    d. A good feeling all around.

2. When you get super-scared during a movie, you think:

    a. "This is a good time to go and get popcorn."

    b. "Where's the action?"

    c. "When is the DVD coming out? I'll want to see this again!"

    d. "I'd rather be watching something foreign and arty."

3. Your favorite actress . . .

    a. Is known for performing all her own stunts.

    b. Is really funny on talk shows.

    c. Is great at acting terrified.

    d. Has been dead for many years.

4. If you were in a movie, your leading man would be . . .

    a. A big hunky black belt in karate.

    b. A guy who'd make you laugh until you peed in your pants.

    c. A dude who'd scare the living night-lights outta you.

    d. A multiple Academy Award–winning actor.

HERE'S HOW YOU SCORED:

Mostly As: You crave action and adventure—in the movies and maybe in your life, too. You like being at the edge of your seat, and love the rush of a chase scene. Some friends accuse you of liking too many "boy" movies, but you're like: "What?! When did boys get a monopoly on thrillers?!"

Mostly Bs: You love to laugh, and comedies are your thing. You've got a healthy funny bone and a great sense of humor. It's not that you don't enjoy other types of movies, but they HAVE to have at least a few laughs to make any flick worthwhile.

Mostly Cs: You like to be TERRIFIED (when you know it's pretend). Scary movies make you feel alive, even if they're all about dead people! You like the tingly feeling you get when you don't know what's on the other side of a door, under the floor, or behind your back.

Mostly Ds: You like old black-and-white movies, arty movies or, basically, any movies that can be called "films." You have good taste, and you can't help it. You're also a tad on the sentimental side. You've probably seen your favorite movie a hundred times. And you never get tired of it. Your friends call you a film buff and that makes you proud.

My TOP TEN fave movies of all time are:

1. _____

2. _____

3. _____

4. _____

5. _____

6. _____

7. _____

8. _____

9. _____

10. _____

Are you big on books?
Find out what your reading reveals.

quiz #29

1. Someone gives you a book for your birthday. You . . .

    a. Wish they had gotten you a better gift than just a book.

    b. Can't wait to crack it open and start reading.

    c. Put it on your bookshelf on top of all the other books you might read someday (but probably won't).

2. The last book you read was . . .

    a. Great because it was short.

    b. Great and you didn't want it to end.

    c. Haven't finished it yet.

3. How many books do you read a month?

    a. 0–1

    b. 5 or more

    c. 2–4

4. Reading is something you . . .

    a. Don't choose to do on your own—ever.

    b. Do all the time—whenever, wherever!

    c. You do if you're really, *really* bored and can't think of anything else to do.

Mostly Bs: You LOVE to read! You love all kinds of stories, and you probably like to write them, too. Nothing makes you more excited than entering some cool new world—a world that may be totally different or very much the same as the one you live in. You've got a hungry imagination, and you've got to feed it with books, books, and more books!

Mostly Cs: You're an okay reader. You really, really like some books, but you don't love when teachers MAKE you read books for homework. You like to come to books when you're in the right mind-set. But keep at it! The more you read, the easier it'll get.

HERE'S HOW YOU SCORED:

Mostly As: All right, sister, it's plain to see that reading is not fundamental for you. You don't know why, really, but you've never understood how people can get excited about books, and sometimes it's a struggle just to get through one. Maybe reading doesn't come easy. Just make sure to ask for help if you're having trouble.

Can you plan your best day ever?

quiz #30

What would the best day of your life be like?

_____

_____

_____

Where would you go?

_____

_____

_____

What would you do?

_____

_____

_____

Who would you bring?

_____

_____

_____

What would you listen to?

_____

_____

_____

What books would you take?

_____

_____

_____

What movies would you see?

_____

_____

_____

the why of me

chapter seven: how smart is your heart?

Usually when people talk about somebody being smart, they mean brainy. Like my mom has this huge IQ, and she can multiply gigantor numbers in her head so fast, it makes me dizzy. So everybody says she's smart, because she's really good with numbers and does really well on tests.

But when you think about it, there are lotsa different ways to be smart. Like my dad is really bad at math. Supposedly, he even got an F in algebra. But my dad reads non-stop and can quote Shakespeare and tell you all kinds of weird facts about history and stuff.

Then there's my cat, Chile Pepper. She's really smart about how I'm feeling. Like the other day, I was really sad because I found out that my friend Luisa is moving to Los Angeles. So I went to my room and started reading a book to get my mind off everything. Next thing I knew, Chile Pepper ran right up into my lap and started rubbing her head under my chin, like she knew I was upset and wanted to make me feel better. And she actually did make me feel better! So then I realized, Chile Pepper is really smart in her heart. She knows when I'm happy or scared or upset, and she knows what to do about it.

Then I started wondering: Is there a way to find out how smart

are at understanding what you're feeling, what everyone else is feeling, and what you can do to help yourself and your friends feel better. Like, these tests revealed that my best friend, Jasmine, avoids people when she's mega-stressed or weirded out. So, last week at school when she walked right past me without even saying hello, I was like, "Oh my God! That is so rude!" until I remembered that she AVOIDS people when she's upset. So I used my emotional intelligence to figure out that she was probably all worked up about something. Then my mom told me that her grandma was sick. So instead of being all mad and nasty because she had avoided me, I called her that night to ask how her gram was feeling and to tell her I was thinking about her. Well, that got Jasmine talking, and she told me how she was feeling kind of sad and a little scared. Before you knew it, she was feeling better. So in the end, I think I was able to cheer her up a bit. It's good to be smart in the heart!

you are in your heart? Just like you take IQ tests to test how brainy you are? It turns out you can actually test what's called your Emotional Intelligence. And it has nothing to do with how good you are at math, science, history, or any subject you get tested on at school. Emotional intelligence is about how good you

Pssst!
The answers for Quizzes 31 through 34 are on page 78. So take all four at once to figure out your emotional intelligence.

Do you groove on your moods?
Or are you baffled by your own self? Measure your me.

quiz #31

1. You're all bummed out and sad but you don't know why. Do you:

    a. Take a good look inside to figure out what the heck's goin' on?

    b. Try to think about lunch, or some cool shoes, or your dog, or anything besides what might be bugging you?

2. You're crazy bored. Do you:

    a. Figure out some way, somehow, to have some fun?

    b. Sit around wishing you had something cool to do?

3. You've got a big test tomorrow, and you've studied really, really hard, but you're still kind of twitchy. Do you:

    a. Call your best friend because you know she'll calm you down?

    b. Study until your eyes cross and your head starts rolling around randomly on your neck?

4. You're mad at your pal. Do you:

    a. Call her up and explain how mad you are and why, and have a nice long chat about it?

    b. NOT call her up because you're so mad and you don't want to listen to anything she has to say?

Are you cool with people's moods or will your mom's fit get you in a snit? Get the lowdown on how much others get you down.

quiz #32

1. Your mom's in a badbadbadbad mood. Do you:

    a. Walk right up to her and ask if there's any way to chill her ill?

    b. Stay as far away as humanly possible until after the storm passes?

2. Your best friend is avoiding you. Do you:

    a. Go out of your way to find her and ask: What's goin' on?!

    b. Go out of your way to avoid her AT ALL COSTS?

3. You're at a party and you don't know anybody. Do you:

    a. Hang out in the back and watch before you try to fit yourself in?

    b. Try to act cool and hope no one'll notice that you're uncomfortable?

4. Your teacher punishes your whole class for misbehaving. Do you:

    a. Sit there thinking, "Wow, it must really be hard to be a teacher"?

    b. Get mad because you know you didn't do anything wrong and it's totally unfair?

Can you talk to your friends and family about what's REALLY going on when something's REALLY going on? Take the talk test.

quiz #33

1. Your mom and dad have a big fight and you're all super-upset about it. Do you:

    a. Tell your mom how weirded out you are?

    b. Go straight to your room and plug your earphones in and zone out?

2. All your friends get invited to a mad-cool party. Except you! Do you:

    a. Call your best friend and tell her exactly how you feel about it?

    b. Walk around acting like you couldn't care any less?

3. You get back a big test from your teacher, and to your surprise and horror, there's a big D on it! Do you:

    a. Wait till after school and tell your teacher you're a little freaked out and ask if her if she can help you do better?

    b. Pray that nobody will EVER find out?

4. You wake up feeling like the loser of the universe. Do you:

    a. Call your best friend and let her turn your frown upside down?

    b. Take it out on your mother/father/brother/sister/pet (not necessarily in that order!)?

If your best friend is bent outta shape, can you help bend her back? Rate your response ratio.

quiz #34

1. A friend tells you she doesn't want to hang out with you anymore. Do you:

    a. Figure out that she must be really upset and ask if you two can talk it out?

    b. Tell her to bug off because you're too good for her anyway?

2. It gets back to you that a few of your "best buddies" think you're a bit of a dweeb. Do you:

    a. Remind yourself that you're not a dweeb, and that you need to find some new friends?

    b. Wonder what you can do to change their minds?

3. Your best friend calls and starts bawling her head off on the phone. Do you:

    a. Let her unload then tell her you totally understand and remind her about the time you bawled your head off?

    b. Try to change the subject and make her feel better that way?

4. Your dad goes off on you for no reason and it's TOTALLY unfair. Do you:

    a. Try to figure out what's bugging him and making him act so crazy?

    b. Tell him he's a mean, hateful person?

OKAY, NOW ADD UP YOUR ANSWERS:

If you got more As than Bs, you're quite comfy with feelings: yours and everybody else's. You're pretty much in touch with your emotions, and you like to rely on your heart to tell you what to do. You're a very secure person, and you value your friendships A LOT. You like to get to the bottom of what's bugging people, or what makes people tick. You'd make an awesome psychiatrist or social worker. And if you have kids, you'll be one of those moms that's really cool to be around because they just "know" how kids feel.

If you got more Bs than As, you use your brain to figure things out more than your heart. It's not that you don't have a huge heart, but your head just automatically takes over when things are stressful. You tend to avoid confrontations because you prefer to work things out in your mind instead of talking things through. Sometimes, when your heart gets hurt, you react by pushing the hurt away instead of working it out. You're every bit as sensitive as the next person, but you don't like to show your vulnerable side even to your closest friends.

How would you describe your personality?

quiz #35

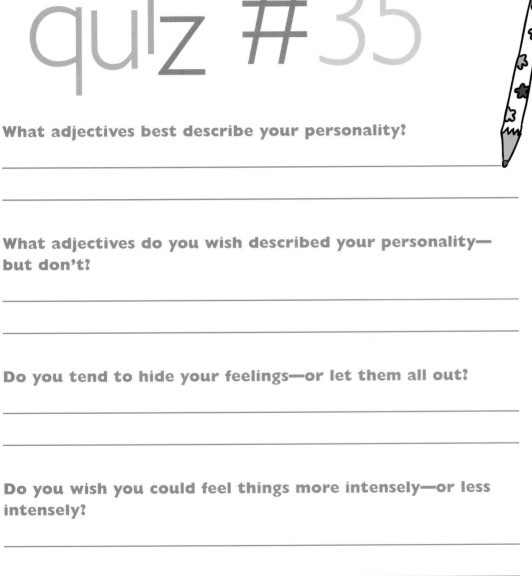

What adjectives best describe your personality?

_____

_____

What adjectives do you wish described your personality— but don't?

_____

_____

Do you tend to hide your feelings—or let them all out?

_____

_____

Do you wish you could feel things more intensely—or less intensely?

_____

_____

chapter eight: the reality of your personality

What do you wanna be when you grow up?" I'm so sick of people asking me this question! My grandpa is 72, and he still doesn't know what he wants to be! But I did start thinking about what kinda job would make me happy someday.

I found out from my uncle Mac that there's a test you can take to help figure out what kinda personality you have, so you can match it up with a job you'd like and be good at. Mac was working as a computer dude at this really cool company. He was doing what he wanted to do, but he still wasn't totally happy and didn't know why. His company convinced him to take this test because they didn't want him to quit. Turns out, he's a people person. He likes being around people, but in the job he had he was working by himself—all day long! So his company changed his job a bit to make use of his people skills—and now he totally loves it.

A mom and daughter named Katherine Cook Briggs and Isabel Briggs Myers invented the test my uncle took, which is called the Myers-Briggs test. Here's my version; I'll tell you what it all means afterward.

Are you a social butterfly or do you like the party to come to you? Get a handle on how you handle others.

quiz #36

1. It's a normal weekend. Do you:

    E. Spend as much hang-and-chill time as possible with your pals?

    I. Look forward to some quality alone-time with me, myself, and I?

2. It's your best friend's birthday. Do you:

    E. Throw her a big crazy surprise party?

    I. Invite her to do something special just with you?

3. It's time to do some back-to-school shopping. Do you:

    E. Call all your friends and see who wants to go with you?

    I. Go solo?

4. You've got a big science test tomorrow. Do you:

    E. Call as many classmates as you can to find out what they're studying?

    I. Try to figure out, on your own, what's going to be on the test?

5. If you had to choose one or the other, you would rather be:

    E. A politician.

    I. An artist.

TALLY UP YOUR SCORE:

If you got more Es, write the letter E in the box below.

If you got more Is, write the letter I in the box below.

And remember, I'll tell you what this all means later.

Marvelous & Fabulous Me   81

Do you think in a straight line or a curlicue?
Pinpoint your logic locator.

quiz #37

1. There's a nasty book report you have to write for school. Do you:

S. Hit the Internet, surf the Web, crack the books, and write a crackerjack outline before you start writing?

N. Read the book and then just dive right into the report, winging it as you go?

2. You're sitting in math class. Do you:

S. Zone in on the teacher and take notes so you can remember every word?

N. Find your mind wandering out the window where there's a cloud that looks like your mom's favorite purse?

3. Your friend has a doozy of a whopper of a problem. Do you:

S. Get a handle on the facts and help her work her way through her problem?

N. Get swept up in the crazy roller coaster of emotions and go up and down with her?

4. You got a cool new jigsaw puzzle for your birthday. Do you:

S. First turn all the pieces right-side up, then separate the pieces that make up the edge, then put these together before tackling any other part of the puzzle?

N. Dump out all the pieces on the floor and just start wherever with whatever and see where it takes ya?

5. You want to re-create a delicious dip your friend made last week, but she's not home. Do you:

S. Look through all the cookbooks in the house to try to find a similar recipe?

N. Pull out all the possible ingredients and start mixing and tasting, mixing and tasting, till you get it right?

TALLY UP YOUR SCORE.

If you got more Ss, write the letter S in the box below.

If you got more Ns, write the letter N in the box below.

Do you listen to your heart or your head?
Uncover who's the captain of your ship.

quiz #38

1. You're invited to two parties you totally wanna go to, but they're on the same night. Do you:

> T. Go to the party you were invited to first because it's the right thing to do and you've gotta do the right thing?

> F. Go to the party where you'll have the most funfunfun?

2. Your brother or sister does something stupid and gets grounded by your parents. Do you:

> T. Figure they deserve whatever they get since they broke the rules?

> F. Feel bad for them even though they totally messed up?

3. You're window-shopping and you expertly spot an expensive necklace you know your best friend would love. Do you:

> T. Almost buy it for her, then decide that you really can't afford it?

> F. Buy now and ask questions later because you know it will make her so happy?

4. A totally adorable stray dog without a collar comes to your front door. Do you:

> T. Make signs and put them up, then go all over the neighborhood till you find the owner?

> F. Beg and beg and beg your parents to let you keep it?

5. You find out that your best friend told you a white lie to protect your feelings. Do you:

    T. Get mad because you hate it when people lie, no matter what the reason?

    F. Thank her for being so considerate?

Do you need order in the court?
Uncover if you'd rather be the judge or the jury.

quiz #39

1. Would you rather be:

    J. A boss?

    P. An employee?

2. Two of your friends are totally going at each other. Do you:

    J. Sit there, trying to figure out who's right and who's wrong?

    P. Nod your head because you can see both sides?

3. You're hosting a PJ party in a few weeks. Do you:

    J. Figure out your music playlists, pick what games you'll play, and plan what movies you'll watch long before the night rolls around?

    P. Wait till everybody shows up, and scope the vibe before you decide what to play?

4. Your social studies teacher is looking for people to lead study groups. Do you:

    J. Jump at the chance and throw up your hand to volunteer?

    P. Hang back and try to fade into the woodwork so you don't get picked?

5. Your teacher picked you to be the leader of your science study group. Do you:

    J. Create assignment sheets to make sure everybody does what they're supposed to do?

    P. Just go about your business, and trust that everyone will take care of theirs, and that it'll all work out A-OK?

TALLY UP YOUR SCORE.

If you got more Js, write the letter J in the box below.

If you got more Ps, write the letter P in the box below.

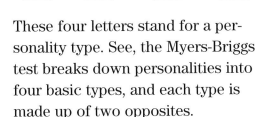

Okay, so now I'm gonna tell you what it all means. You know how you put a letter in each of the boxes at the end of the last four quizzes? Now put each letter in the four boxes below.

These four letters stand for a personality type. See, the Myers-Briggs test breaks down personalities into four basic types, and each type is made up of two opposites.

INTROVERT AND EXTROVERT

I is for Introvert. An introvert is all about looking inside, being kinda shy, a bit of a lone wolf, keeping to yourself, and liking your alone-time. If there's a crowd, you like to be hanging in the shadows of it.

E is for Extrovert. An extrovert likes being around people. Going out with them. Staying home with them. If there's a crowd, extroverts like to be right in the middle of it.

SENSING AND INTUITION

S is for Sensing. Just the facts, only the facts, and all the facts. That's what makes sense to people who like to use their sense. Not to mention that logic is their best friend.

N is for Intuition (we used up the I for Introvert, in case you're wondering. . . .) If you tend to know things because you get a funny feeling, or you

decide things based on wild inspirations or leaps of your imagination, then you're an intuition gal.

THINKING AND FEELING

T is for Thinking. Reasoning things out and considering stuff long and hard makes thinkers happy. They also like to know if something is true or false.

F is for Feeling. Trusting and using your heart and guts more than your brain to decide things and guide you makes you a feeler. You're not as concerned about whether something is true or false, but rather if it's better or worse.

JUDGING AND PERCEIVING

J is for Judging. Organization and order are the order of the day when you've got the personality to judge.

P is for Perceiving. Are you comfy with chaos? Or maybe hanging loose and going with the flow makes you happy? Then you've got good perception skills.

So now here comes the fun part. If you mix 'n' match all these personality types (which you know is what I love doing best!) you get a total of 16 possible personality types. So the letters in the boxes are YOUR uniquely YOU personality type. Find the letters that match yours and see what personality type YOU are!

ENFJ. You appreciate and celebrate other people. You tend to gogogo and want to leave the world a better place than you found it. You're a regular Miss Congeniality who likes to lead, but also plays nicely with others. You also like to join lots of clubs. ENFJs make great **psychiatrists, party planners, and politicians,** and do well in other jobs where communication and appreciation top the to-do list.

ENFP. You're all about ch-ch-ch-changes. Your energy and enthusiasm are outrageous and contagious. You drip charisma and love talking the talk as well as walking the walk. You're a dreamer and a doer and spend lots of time thinking about all the amazing things that could happen in your life. ENFPs make great **painters, entrepreneurs, and reporters,** and do well in other jobs where enthusiastic curiosity is your success secret.

INFJ. You tend to be a solo flyer and a lone wolf. You want to understand. Yourself. Everybody else. The world. You prefer a small tea party to a ball. You want harmony and tend to be a little quiet and gentle. You never give up and always show up on time. INFJs make great **scientists, psychologists, and musicians,** and do well in other jobs where inspiration and imagination work in wonderful collaboration.

INFP. You don't get right in other people's faces, but you do get things done. You're good at organizing people without seeming too bossy and you don't ask for help too much. You've also got a wild side and can be quite saucy! You prefer a small cool crew to hang with, but you don't make it easy to get to know you. INFPs make great **writers, teachers, and political activists,** and do well in other jobs that help make you and me be whoever we wanna be.

ENTJ. You look things right in the eye and deal with them right here, right now. You analyze, strategize, conceptualize, theorize, and take charge. You don't like following orders but like giving them. You win spelling bees and science fairs. And you're a mega mover and shaker. ENTJs make great **CEOs, labor organizers, and bankers,** and do well in other jobs where anyone can see strategy is key.

ENTP. You're complicated. You think quick on your feet and always get the job done. You hate a rut, it drives you nuts. You like to figure out newer, better ways of doing stuff. You're clever and flexible and don't mind taking a few risks, cutting a few corners, and getting by on your wits. ENTPs make great **entrepreneurs, inventors, and architects,** and do well in other jobs where innovation and creation get you a standing ovation.

INTJ. You play your cards close to your vest. You're quick and sharp, but other people don't always know this about you. You don't take no for an answer. You're kinda the strong, silent type who makes your own rules. You'd rather get straight As than get invited to all the cool parties. People call you a bookworm, but you're also an early bird who often catches the big juicy worm. INTJs make great **engineers, professors, and judges,** and do well in other jobs where seeing the big picture is no small thing.

INTP. You can do your homework in an earthquake. You're a great challenger of Truth. You seem kinda under the radar, but your mind's always working, working, working, even though it sometimes looks like you're on a planet far, far away. You know what's hot and what's not. And you love a juicy mystery. INTPs make great **physicists, mathematicians, and computer animators,** and do well in other jobs where logic rules and asking "why?" is what it's all about.

ESTJ. You see a job, figure out how to do it, and then do it. You can see two steps ahead, and tweak your plans accordingly. You watch with an eagle eye to make sure everything that has to get done gets done. You love calendars and schedules, and you really enjoy crossing stuff off your to-do lists. ESTJs make **great managers, salespeople, and detectives,** and do well in other jobs where it's a ton of fun to see things through to the end.

ESFJ. You dig peace and harmony. And, for you, order is the order of the day. Reliability, dependability, responsibility, cooperation—you just want everyone to get along.

You like to be liked. A good listener, you sometimes have to work at not being too helpful. ESFJs make great **nurses, teachers, and social workers,** and do well in other jobs where helping and cooperation are part of an organization.

ISTJ. You like facts, figures, and systems. Your fingers tend to get worked to the bone, and you almost always look before you leap. You like rules and enjoy following them. New people make you a little skittish, but once you get comfy, you like to do group things. And you even volunteer to do chores! ISTJs make great **accountants, policewomen, and dentists,** and do well in other jobs where thorough thoughtfulness and thoughtful thoroughness go hand-in-hand with perseverance.

ISFJ. You'll go to the ends of the earth if you're convinced you're doing the right thing. You're generous with sympathy and the last one to toot your own horn. You don't like alotta surprises. You want order and you worry if things change too much or if anyone starts rocking the boat. You like to be behind the scenes. ISFJs make great **interior decorators, counselors, and librarians,** and do well in other jobs where making people's lives prettier, happier, and healthier is all in a day's work.

ESTP. You say what you mean and mean what you say. And if things get a little dull, you're likely to start stirring the pot. You're rambuctalicious, and even though your head's in the clouds, your feet are planted firmly in your no-nonsense shoes. You like life action-packed and high-energy. You also like nice stuff and like to keep your nice stuff nice. ESTPs make great **marketers, race car drivers, and farmers,** and do well in other jobs that take fast reactions and put you in the middle of the action.

ESFP. You're the life of the party and draw people to you like a juicy

bone in a room full of hungry hounds. You love to give, but sometimes it's not so easy for you to receive. You've got a strong shoulder to cry on, and you're always there to "ooh" and "aah" over the cool new blue your friend painted her room. If anything, you get too excited and sometimes have trouble keeping your train on one track. ESFP's make great **comedians, fashion designers, and photographers,** and do well in other jobs where it helps to have an eye and an ear for everything and everyone around you.

ISTP. You fly by the seat of your pants. You're there whenever your friend's in a pinch, pickle, or jam. You're a people watcher and you like to know what makes you and everything else tick. Don't be surprised if you find you're drawn to extreme sports or solving intricate riddles. You're also a reasonable realist. ISTPs make great **pilots, athletes, and firefighters,** and do well in other jobs where it's important to keep a cool head while everyone else is getting hot under the collar.

ISFP. You hate it when everyone's not having fun. And you'll do whatever it takes to make sure everybody's A-OK, but you never seem to hog the spotlight. It's hard not to like you. You love making special homemade CDs or cool bracelets as gifts for your pals. Sometimes you blend into the scenery, but just because you're not making a lot of noise, doesn't mean you don't get stuff done. You also make a top-drawer referee. ISFPs make great **veterinarians, forest rangers, and naturalists,** and do well in other jobs where you mother Mother Nature.

Can you predict your friends' futures?
Use the Myers-Briggs types to help you
figure out who's gonna be what.

quiz #40

Here's all you gotta do: Let's say your BFF seems like an ESTP. Check out the jobs listed with her profile and see which fits her best. Then fill in the info below.

In 20 years, you can check back to see if you were right!

_____ = _____
Friend's name   Job name

_____ = _____
Friend's name   Job name

_____ = _____
Friend's name   Job name

_____ = _____
Friend's name   Job name

_____ = _____
Your name   Job name

What job would float your boat?

quiz #41

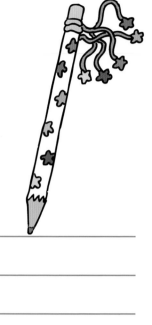

What jobs do YOU think you'd be good at?

_____

_____

_____

What jobs do you think you would hate?

_____

_____

_____

Do you care a lot about money?
Will it help you determine what job you get?

_____

_____

_____

chapter nine:

enneagram anyone?

Do you ever wonder why certain stuff totally makes sense to you, and other stuff makes your eyes cross and your brain turn to mushy oatmeal? Take my sister's room. It's so neat, it makes a pin look messy. Like EVERYTHING's all put away and tidied up. It feels like the whole room's being strangled. Like you can't breathe in there. But my sister loves it. And so does my mom. My room, on the other hand, is often called a "pig sty," "disaster zone," and a "disgusting, disorganized mess." But to me, my room looks exciting. Like I'm a mad scientist and my clothes, books, and magic markers are part of some cool experiment. So how is it possible that people who are related to one another can think so differently?

I recently found out about this thing called the Enneagram. You say it like this: EN-E-uh-gram. It's a way to figure out what kind of personality you have. And to understand the personalities of everyone around you. Like your mom and dad, your sisters and brothers, your teachers and, of course, your friends. This way you don't have to get all mad cranky just because someone is different from you.

The Enneagram goes back hundreds of years, to the Middle East. It was supposedly invented by these guys called Sufis, these crazy cool dudes who used to go into trances to write poems. They also did this dance where they would twirl around and around in circles REALLY fast till they got all kooky. Once, after I ate all these syrupy sweet cookies and ice cream and was on a sensational sugar high, my mom said, "Stop acting like a whirling dervish! You're giving me a headache." I had no idea what in the whole wide world she meant, but it turns out that's what a lot of Sufis were called because of their twirling. Since I already write poems, and I can twirl with the best of them, I'm pretty sure I could be a super Sufi.

Okay, now back to the Enneagram. See the drawing on the next page? This is how the Sufi dudes drew the Enneagram. See how it has nine points around the circle? Those nine points stand for nine different personality types. If you're like me, you might think, "There are 25 kids in my class, and they all seem to have totally different personalities." But the Sufi dudes noticed (kind of like Myers and Briggs) that there are actually lots of similarities between people. They were able to narrow all those personality types down to nine:

1. **The Perfectionist**
2. **The Helper**
3. **The Performer**
4. **The Artist**
5. **The Rationalist**
6. **The Questioner**
7. **The Adventurer**
8. **The Boss**
9. **The Peacemaker**

And once I saw the nine, it all started to make sense to me. Now you're gonna figure out which is your personality type. But here's a tip: You may be a combination of two or even three personalities.

Crazy as it sounds, at some time in our lives, we've all been all nine personality types!

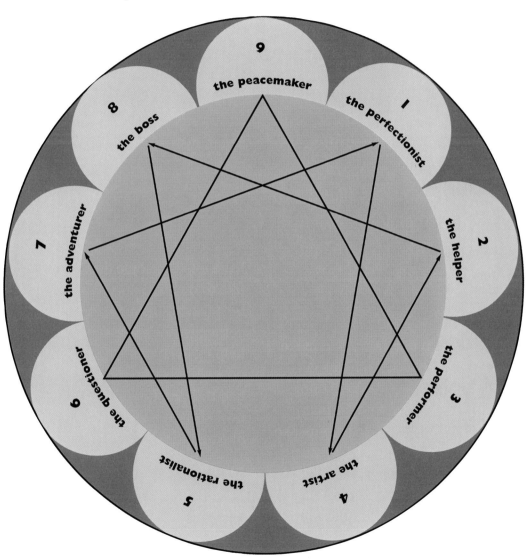

Are you obsessed with perfection, helplessly helpful, or antsy for adventure?

quiz #42

For each Enneagram personality type, rate yourself on a scale of 1 to 10, with 10 being "I am definitely like this" and 1 being "I am not at all like this."

1. The Perfectionist:

Perfectionists like to try and make everything perfect. And they get kinda snarky and tweaky if things don't go according to their plan. They like to have everything just so. Mistakes really bug perfectionists. My sister is a total perfectionist. Which explains a lot. And it makes me see what's perfect about my sister, instead of what's perfectly annoying.

Rating ____

2. The Helper:

Helpers like to have lots of people around and they like to do good deeds for others. My best friend, Jasmine, is a helper. In ceramics, she's sometimes so busy helping everyone else that she doesn't finish her own project. I feel bad that she doesn't just do her own stuff, but she really seems to like helping others.

Rating ____

3. The Performer: Performers like to decide to do something, and then they work and work and work until they make the thing happen. My cousin Lydia is like this. She's won every science fair from Kalamazoo to Timbuktu. She'll get some crazy idea—like how to make roofs out of recycled soda cans—and then she'll just figure out how to do it.

Rating ____

4. The Artist: Artists feel deep things, ultra deeply, and they long for things they can't quite ever get. My cat, Chile Pepper, has an artist's personality. She always longs for more food than we give her and yowls when she doesn't get it. And she wants to be in all the places she's not allowed and will sometimes try to bite—even me—when I tell her no.

Rating ____

5. The Rationalist: Rationalists think and think and think. They try to solve all their problems and figure everything out by thinking. My dad's a rationalist. He'll be sitting in his big corduroy chair in his office, with his eyebrows all smashed and scrunched. I'll say, "Dad, whatya doin'?" And he'll always just say, "Thinking." But at least when he tells you something, you know he's thought a lot about it.

Rating ____

6. The Questioner: Questioners worry about everything that could go wrong. They want to be safe and secure, and they think that the more info they have, the better they'll feel. My friend Tara is a major questioner. When you go to the movies with her, she's always asking, "Who is that?" "Is she going to die?" "Is everything gonna be okay?" Sometimes I make up answers just to yank her chain.

Rating ____

7. The Adventurer:

Adventurers always wanna have fun. Fabulous freaky fun. They always wanna take off in some bold new direction. In addition to being an Artist, Chile Pepper is also an adventurer. I always see her darting off in one direction or another. And sometimes I'll find her climbing up some huge tree. I love that she thinks of our backyard as her very own jungle.

Rating ____

8. The Boss: Bosses are strong and they're always standing up for what they believe in and what they need. They want to be the one in charge, telling everyone what to do. My mom's a boss. She not only likes—she LOVES—telling everyone what to do (including yours truly). And everyone seems to listen.

Rating ____

9. The Peacemaker:

Peacemakers always wanna smooth things over, make everything okay, get everybody to compromise. My English teacher, Ms. Radcliffe, is a great peacemaker. This kid in my class called Thumper (that's his nickname, his real name is Forrest) is always arguing and getting in fights with another kid in my class, Joseph, who is louder than loud. But Ms. Radcliffe somehow calms them both down and makes everybody feel okay.

Rating ____

S o, which was your highest rating? That's the personality type you THINK you are.

Write it down here:

_____

Now let's see if that matches the results of the next quiz.

Are your ratings right? Find out by putting yourself in these everyday situations that are sure to reveal your true personality.

quiz #43

Circle only the answer that applies to you, even if that means not choosing an answer to some questions.

1. You have a huge part in the school play. When you wake up the morning of the show, do you:

A. Feel psyched because you know you're gonna totally rock?

B. Say, "What the heck! I've done my best and learned my lines. What else can I do?"

C. Tell your mom and dad that you're having such a blast in the play that you wanna be an actor?

D. Get yourself all worked up because you're totally sure you're gonna mess everything up?

2. It's the first day of a new school year. Do you:

E. Make yourself swear that you're gonna get As, and nothing but As?

F. Hope you and your crew are gonna have a great year?

G. Keep your fingers crossed that your teacher will really like you and you'll get to be her pet?

H. Volunteer to be teacher's helper, erase the chalkboard after class, and carry boxes when he's overloaded?

3. Tomorrow, you're leaving for sleepaway camp for the first time. Do you:

I. Wish that you hadn't signed up in the first place and feel you've made a mistake?

B. Pack as many books as possible in your duffle bag?

H. Start daydreaming about all the cool new people you'll meet and fun friends you'll make?

D. Have to stop your brain from worrying about who your bunk mate will be and whether your counselor will like you?

4. Your parents are all packed up and going to Europe for a week. Do you:

E. Worry that your regular schedule will be interrupted?

A. Get excited about being your own boss 24/7?

G. Beg your mom to bring you a souvenir from Paris to show your friends?

C. Make a mental list of all the junk food you're going to eat?

5. When your mom and dad make suggestions for a school report, do you:

A. Try to convince them that they are wrong and your way is better?

F. Appreciate their suggestions and thank them for helping you?

I. Feel that your parents don't understand the way you think?

D. Feel hurt because your parents are picking on you?

6. Your teacher accuses you of passing a note to your friend. Do you:

B. Shrug and figure you didn't mean any harm?

G. Feel embarrassed that your teacher scolded you in front of the class?

H. Talk to all your friends about it at recess?

C. Make a joke out of it?

7. Your mother grounds you for talking back, and you were planning on going to the movies with your friends. Do you:

    A. Argue with your mother until she gives in?

    I. Feel as if your mother really doesn't get you?

    F. Take your punishment and tell your mother you will try to behave better in the future?

    H. Call your friends and ask if they'll wait until you can go with them?

8. Your teacher announces that instead of giving a test, each student will tell a story. Do you:

    D. Feel really nervous about speaking in front of the class?

    G. Feel excited because you love getting up in front of the class?

    B. Figure that you already learned the material for the test, so it doesn't matter?

    I.   Ask if you can recite a poem instead?

9. You are taking piano lessons. Do you:

    C. Practice a little and then invent some new tunes?

    E. Practice the same piece over and over until you get it right?

    A. Practice only the pieces you like?

    G. Learn even more pieces than your teacher assigned?

10. On a road trip with your family, do you:

    H. Buy souvenirs for all your friends?

    B. Not pay much attention to the scenery because you're reading a book?

    F. Go along with what everybody else wants to do?

    A. Wish you were old enough to drive?

11. Your mother is redecorating the living room. Do you:

    B. Let her do her thing?

    I. Wish she wouldn't change anything because you'll miss the old room?

    D. Worry that you won't feel comfortable in the new room?

    E. Go shopping with her because you don't want her to make any mistakes?

12. You're going to get a haircut. Do you:

  E. Look in all the magazines to see which would be the perfect cut for you?

  A. Tell the hairstylist exactly how to cut your hair?

  F. Ask your friends and family what style they think would look good on you?

  H. Get the hairstyle most of your friends have?

13. If you walk to school, do you:

  I. Take the prettiest route?

  C. See how many different routes you can discover?

  F. Agree to the route your friends have chosen?

  D. Always walk with your friends?

14. Are you happiest when:

  B. Everybody leaves you alone?

  E. You've checked everything off your to-do list?

  G. You've won a race or gotten the best grade in the class?

  D. You have nothing to worry about?

15. You are happiest:

  H. Spending time with your friends.

  C. Going on an adventure.

  G. When somebody gives you a compliment.

  I. When you have a best friend who understands you.

16. You are most upset when:

  A. People don't listen to your great advice.

  E. You make a mistake.

  F. Your friends or family are fighting.

  D. You have to do something new.

17. When you are unhappy, do you:

  G. Put on a good face so nobody will know?

  B. Get absorbed in a good novel?

  E. Think of all the things you've done wrong?

  H. Talk to all your friends about it?

18. Your two best friends are having a fight. Do you:

    C. Try to make them laugh?

    F. Help them make up?

    D. Worry that they'll blame you?

    I. Feel lonely because you're left out?

19. Before you go to bed at night, do you:

    G. Count how many parties you're invited to over the weekend?

    A. Think about all you've accomplished that day?

    E. Lay out your clothes and books for the next day?

    H. Decide which friends you'll invite over on the weekend?

20. When you're at a party, do you:

    B. Enjoy watching the way everybody acts?

    F. Try to help everybody have a good time?

    I. Feel that you have nothing in common with the other kids?

    C. Have a great time because you love parties?

SCORES:

If more of your answers are **A** than any other letter, you are probably a **Boss.**

If more of your answers are **B** than any other letter, you are probably a **Rationalist.**

If more of your answers are **C** than any other letter, you are probably an **Adventurer.**

If more of your answers are **D** than any other letter, you are probably a **Questioner.**

If more of your answers are **E** than any other letter, you are probably a **Perfectionist.**

If more of your answers are **F** than any other letter, you are probably a **Peacemaker.**

If more of your answers are **G** than any other letter, you are probably a **Performer.**

If more of your answers are **H** than any other letter, you are probably a **Helper.**

If more of your answers are **I** than any other letter, you are probably an **Artist.**

Can you find a match for each personality?

quiz #44

Go through your friends, family, enemies, and frenemies and fill in a name for each Enneagram type!

1. The Perfectionist = _____

2. The Helper = _____

3. The Performer = _____

4. The Artist = _____

5. The Rationalist = _____

6. The Questioner = _____

7. The Adventurer = _____

8. The Boss = _____

9. The Peacemaker = _____

Does your personality fit nicely into a box?
Or do you have a foot in several?

quiz #45

Why hat do you love about your personality? What do you hate?
Tell me!

What are three things that you really wanna change?
(Don't be too hard on yourself!)

1. _____

2. _____

3. _____

What are three things about your personality that you
really, REALLY like? (Don't be modest now!)

1. _____

2. _____

3. _____

chapter ten: what's in your stars?

My cat, Chile Pepper, was born in early September. She's a total neat freak and she's obsessed with the tidiness of her litter box. It can't be the least bit dirty. If there's any poop in it, she refuses to go in and pitches a meowing fit. Chile Pepper's also a worrier. My mom says that she waits by the door until I get home from school. But as soon as I walk in, she acts all normal and wants back-scratches and chin-rubs.

The weird thing is that my friend Ruth is exactly like Chile Pepper (except for the part about back-scratches and chin-rubs) and they have the exact same birthday. So I started to wonder, is this a coincidence?

Turns out that on the great and glorious moment when you are born, the stars and the planets all line up in a way that is totally unique to you. Woo-hoo! Don't you feel special? I know I do. Your astrological chart—which shows exactly which planet was where at your birth—is kinda like a snowflake. It's completely unique, yet shares lots of similarities with other people's charts.

You may already know what your "sign" is. Astrologers call this your "sun sign." There are 12 sun signs all together and they pretty much match up with the months of the year. People who have the same sign—like my friend Ruth and Chile Pepper (Okay, she's a cat, but I think of her as a person), who are both Virgos—may have similar characteristics.

But your sun sign is just one part of astrology. You also have what're called a moon sign and a rising sign. For example, your sun sign may be Gemini, but your moon may be in Aries and your rising sign in Taurus. Okay, but what does it all mean?

Well, your sun sign is the go-for-it part of yourself. It describes things like what you wanna be when you grow up, and how you're gonna make your dreams come true. Your moon sign is all about your inner world of emotions and feelings. It's how you really, really feel inside that part of you that no

one else can see. Like how happy you feel when you get a compliment or how bad you feel when you see someone get hurt. And your rising sign is all about your personality. Like the way people see you from the outside.

The cool thing about astrology is that it can help you figure out who you are. It can help you understand why you're frustrated by certain things, and why people can be frustrated by you. I'm gonna tell you more about your sun signs (and if you don't know yours, I've listed the dates they cover beside them, so you can figure it out). I've also put a Zany Zodiac poster in this box so you can hang it on your wall and have a handy way to keep tabs on everyone's sun sign!

Unfortunately, I can't tell you what your moon or rising signs are because I'd need to know more about you than the day of your birth. I'd need to know where you were born, the exact time, and the year. But YOU can try to figure out what your moon and rising signs are by taking the next quiz!

quiz #46

Here you'll find all the descriptions of the zodiac sun signs. As you read through them, first rate them on a scale of 1 to 10 to see how closely they resemble your emotional self. If it's a 1, then that sign doesn't resemble what's going on inside you at all. If it's a 9 or 10, well, that's probably your moon sign. Then do the same for your rising sign. Remember, the rising sign is all about how you think other people see you, and that's not necessarily how you REALLY are at all!

Aries (March 21 to April 19). You're a pioneer and adventurer. You're always starting new projects, and are pretty peppy and on-the-go. You can be a little me-first-y, so watch out for this part of yourself.

Moon Sign____Rising Sign____

Taurus (April 21 to May 21). You love nature and beautiful things. You like the woods and peace and quiet. You're strong and constant in your feelings, but also sometimes stubborn, so be careful about locking horns with others.

Moon Sign____Rising Sign____

Gemini (May 22 to June 21). You see both sides to everything, which makes you very diplomatic, but you have a tough time deciding stuff. You like to talk and play. One thing you hate: to be kept waiting.

Moon Sign_____ Rising Sign_____

Cancer (June 22 to July 23). You like to care for and feed people. Sometimes even when they're not hungry. You are way sensitive and feel hurt easily, so it's good to stay away from people who are super-critical.

Moon Sign_____ Rising Sign_____

Leo (July 24 to August 23). You're enthusiastic, generous, and fun to hang out with. You like drama—watching it *and* making it. But you can also be quite bossy, which can annoy the people you're bossing.

Moon Sign_____ Rising Sign_____

Virgo (August 24 to September 23). You like everything to have a place, and you like to have a place for everything. You love helping people organize their rooms and their life. You love pets and animals. And you can be a wacky worrywart.

Moon Sign_____ Rising Sign_____

Libra (September 24 to October 23). You like everyone to get along in perfect harmony. Sometimes you can take forever to make up your mind, which can make people (including you!) crazy.

Moon Sign_____ Rising Sign_____

Scorpio (October 24 to November 22). You love secrets. And people can trust you to keep them. You're kind of mysterious because you like to hide who you really are. You're a natural healer, but when you're mad, you're really mad, and your words can sting!

Moon Sign_____ Rising Sign_____

Sagittarius (November 23 to December 21). You are full of big ideas. And you love to travel the ocean blue and see the world around you. You're friendly and fun, but you spend a lot of time thinking about stuff, too. The only thing is, you can be a bit of a flake.

Moon Sign____Rising Sign____

Capricorn (December 22 to January 20). You like to laugh and tell jokes. But sometimes this is to hide what a Gloomy Gus you are inside. You're practical and efficient. You're also like the little engine that could—it might take you a while, but you'll always get there.

Moon Sign____Rising Sign____

Aquarius (January 21 to February 19). You like to go outside the box and around the bend. You're pretty unconventional. You love your freedom and don't wanna be fenced in. The only problem is at times you tend to act like a know-it-all.

Moon Sign____Rising Sign____

Pisces (February 20 to March 20). You tend to have deep and strong emotions. You're also a daydreamer, crazy creative, and sorta messy. You like your quality alone-time, but you also like to hang out and listen to music.

Moon Sign____Rising Sign____

OKAY, NOW IT'S TIME TO TALLY UP. What scored highest for your moon sign? THAT's probably your moon sign.

And what scored highest for your rising sign? THAT's probably your rising sign.

Now fill in all your astrological signs below: your sun sign (the sign you are because of the date you were born), plus your moon sign and your rising sign.

I am a(n) ——————————

with a moon in ——————————

and a(n) —————— ascendent.

(That's the fancy name for rising sign.)

**Now that you know a little more about
the sun, moon, and rising signs . . .**

quiz #47

What signs do you think you'd be best friends with?

_____

_____

_____

Are there any signs that you need to avoid?

_____

_____

_____

Is there a love match somewhere in the stars? Who with?

_____

_____

_____

chapter eleven: what's in your cards?

Jasmine, my best friend, went to a birthday party the other day where she had her fortune told by this amazing lady with a deck of cards called tarot cards (say TAR-o). What she did was pull out certain cards and tell you about what was going on in your life and what might happen in the future. Jasmine said it was really cool and a little spooky because she seemed to know things about people she had no business knowing. Like she told Jasmine she had a friend with a "hot cat." At first Jasmine had no idea what she was talking about. Then she realized it was me. My cat's name is Chile Pepper!

So I started reading all this stuff about the tarot. It turns out tarot decks are at least 600 years old! The earliest tarot cards ever found go back to the Middle Ages, but some people believe the tarot is even older than that! One theory says the tarot cards originated in Ancient Egypt, while another theory says they come from the old mystical system called Kabbalah. The truth is, no one really knows for sure where they're from or how they came about, which I think makes them even cooler.

But to me the kookiest thing about them is this: playing cards (you know, that 52-card deck you play gin rummy and solitaire with?) actually came from the tarot. The names of the cards are a little different, but there are still a lot of similarities, too. Like aces, kings, and queens are the same, but jacks are called "knights." And regular playing cards have four suits: hearts, clubs, spades, and diamonds. So do tarot cards, only theirs are called cups, wands, swords, and pentacles (five-pointed stars). Also, the tarot deck has what are called "Major Arcana" cards. These are cards with names like "The Magician" and "The Emperor." But only one "Major Arcana" made it into modern-day playing card decks. Can you guess which one? Here's a hint: It's not a joke. Get it? Yes, it's the joker!

One of the cool things about Tarot cards is that each suit means something. Wands are all about fire, energy, action; cups are all about water, emotion, love; swords are all about air, ideas, words; pentacles are all about earth, work, and money. And each kind of card means something. Aces are precious and valuable, like jewels or something you treasure. Kings represents wisdom, planning, and strategy. Queens give support and comfort and also negotiate and take care of people. Knights are bold, brave adventurers who can fight their way out of the tightest corners. And there's actually a fifth type of picture card in a tarot deck in addition to the ace, king, queen, and knight, and that's the page card. Page cards are the children cards. They represent four different types of kids—one of which may very well be just like you! Now don't you wanna find out which kinda page card you are?!

Are you the page of cups, wands, swords, or pentacles?
See what suit suits you!

quiz #48

1. When you're at the movies, you . . .
   a. Yell out "Woo-hoo!" when the heroine escapes the bad guy.
   b. Sob your eyes out at the really sad parts.
   c. Look for what parts they left out from the book it's based on.
   d. Think about how fun it would be to work at a movie theater.

2. At your perfect pajama party you would . . .
   a. Spend the night flipping out on a trampoline.
   b. Make up stories about fairies and flying lions living in a strange and beautiful land.
   c. Write mini plays for all your friends.
   d. Make cool crafts that you're going to give as Mother's Day presents.

3. Over summer vacation, you'd love to . . .
   a. Be the captain of your summer soccer league team.
   b. Daydream the days away.
   c. Read a kajillion and one books.
   d. Get a fun job, make some fun money.

4. If your grandparents gave you $20, you'd . . .
   a. Spend it on the very first thing you saw and loved.
   b. Hide it in a place so special that you'd then forget where it was.
   c. Buy a couple extra diaries so you could write down your every thought.
   d. Put it in your bank account with the $500 you've already saved from babysitting.

Mostly As: You are the page of wands.

You're Little Miss Energetic— impulsive, creative, and a born leader. You shine a little light on everyone around you.

Mostly Bs: You are the page of cups.

You're Little Miss Dreamer— emotional, dreamy, and sensitive. Your friends can depend on you to be gentle and kind.

Mostly Cs: You are the page of swords.

You're Little Miss Bookworm— you love to read, write, talk, and think. If someone's got a problem, you'll be sure to help her find a way to fix it.

Mostly Ds: You are the page of pentacles.

You're Little Miss Practical— down-to-earth and an excellent worker bee. Everyone can count on you once you give your word.

quiz #49

If you could, would you want to know what your future holds? Would you want the power to tinker with your own destiny, or would you prefer just to live it? Tell me!

If you could make up your own fortune, what would it be?

_____

_____

_____

_____

_____

_____

_____

_____

If you could, would you want to know what your future holds? What kind of things specifically would you like to know? For instance, do you want to know who you might marry someday, or if you're going to have kids (and how many), or if you're going to be rich and famous? Get specific!

_____

_____

_____

_____

_____

_____

_____

_____

_____

_____

_____

Now use the tarot cards that come in this Quiz Box to help you answer the questions!

take a tarot adventure

The tarot deck in this box can help you answer big life questions and lead you on as many adventures as your mind can imagine. In this deck, you'll find 22 cards made up of four different suits: cups, wands, pentacles, and swords. Each suit has an ace, a king, a queen, a knight, and a page. So that makes 20 cards. The twenty-first card is a wild card. And there's a twenty-second card, too, with a handy reference guide to help you read the cards!

Here's how to create your very own magical mystic quest using the cards to guide you along: First make sure to take the quiz on page 116 to find out what card you are. Then take this card as your starting card. Lay it faceup on the table. Shuffle all the other cards and lay them facedown to the right of your card.

Now you can either start telling a story based on your card, or ask a question about your future (or someone else's). Take a card from the top of the deck that's facedown and lay it faceup below your first card. Read the mini-descriptions included in the deck to figure out what it's all about. Then see if you can uncover how this card relates to your first card. If you asked a question, figure out how this card answered it. Trust your instincts and follow your gut. Tarot is as much about what comes up in your imagination as it is about the literal cards themselves. Each card you pick adds another character to your story until you reach the end of your trip or answer another one of your questions. You can play by yourself or with your friends.

**If you could make your very own world,
what in the world would your world be?**

quiz #50

Imagine a place where you can have anything, eat anything, wear anything, go anywhere, and be anything. Fill in all the blanks and you'll have a perfect description of your ideal life. Show it to your friends and see if they would like to visit your special world. Or maybe they have a paradise of their very own.

My name would be_____.

I'd live in _____.

My house would be made outta_____.

I'd have_____brothers and _____sisters.

I'd get up every day at _____.

I'd go to bed every day at_____.

My bed would be made_____, unmade_____, or made by a maid_____. (Check one.)

Every Tuesday for dinner, I'd eat_____

I'd know how to bake these desserts:

And I'd know how to make these meals:

For pets, I'd have these animals:

I'd go to school_____hours a day.

For a ringtone I'd have

I'd be able to play these instruments:

For summer vacation, I'd go to these places:

To school, I'd wear_____

_____

_____

To bed, I'd wear_____

_____

To a costume ball, I'd wear_____

_____

_____

I'd be a _____when I grew up.

I'd have these foods growing in my garden:_____

_____

_____

And I'd have these flowers growing in my yard:_____

_____

_____

The air would smell like_____.

I'd invent a car that runs on_____.

I'd invite these historical figures to dinner:_____

_____

_____

I'd get these writers to read me their books:_____

_____

_____

I'd have these musicians play one of their songs:_____

_____

_____

I'd be in the Olympics in these sports:_____

_____

_____

I'd get this actor to play me in the movie of my life:_____

_____

I'd get this guitarist to play with me in my band:_____

_____

I'd get to hang out with these cartoon characters:_____

_____

_____

I'd go back to this period in history:_____

I'd discover a cure for_____.

I'd save people's lives by being a _____.

My world would be called _____.

So didya learn anything new about marvelous, fabulous YOU?! Will you be going to the moon or creating your very own toonz? Does maroon make you swoon? Did your stars tell you more about who you are? I sure hope so!

Here's the thing: There's always more to discover about the what, when, where, how, and who of you. So don't stop exploring your likes, dislikes, head, heart, ideas, hopes, and dreams! To help you, I've included a few things in this box you might wanna try.

I already told you about the Tarot Cards and the Zany Zodiac, but check out the Personality Revealer Spinwheel! You can match up your zodiac sign AND your Myers-Briggs personality profile AND your Enneagram personality type to reveal a totally unique description of what kind of person YOU are! I've also included a blank notebook for you to jot down whatever, whenever. This journal can be your special place to find out more about the fabulous, marvelous, kooky, zany person that you are. You'll also find Fortune-Telling Cootie-Catchers: You write in your own fortunes and be a fortune teller for all your friends! As for the stickers, well, those are just for you to enjoy whichever way your heart chooses.

Still hungry for more? Then let me know what subjects you want quizzes on, and what you want to know about yourself. You can e-mail me at lmm@littlemissmatched.com. I'd love to hear from you!

Sadly, it's time for me to say good-bye because there are no more pages left in this book. I hate saying good-bye, but that's because I'm an ENFJ, my moon's in Cancer, I've got heaps of emotional intelligence, and I guess it's just in my cards (now you can see what I learned by taking all these quizzes!). Please remember, to thine own self be true!

Cheers,
LittleMissMatched